Notes for a Guidebook

ams press
new york

NOTES

FOR A

GUIDEBOOK

Lucien Stryk

NEW POETRY SERIES

ALAN SWALLOW

PS
3569
T76
N6
1975

Library of Congress Cataloging in Publication Data

Stryk, Lucien.
    Notes for a guidebook.

    Reprint of the 1965 ed. published by A. Swallow, Denver,
in series: New poetry series.
    I. Title.
[PS3569.T76N6   1975]   811'.5'4   79-179832
ISBN 0-404-56032-6
        0-404-56000-8 (SET)

The New Poetry Series

Reprinted by arrangement with
The Swallow Press Inc.
Copyright © 1965 by Lucien Stryk
First AMS edition published in 1975
AMS Press Inc. 56 E. 13th St.
New York, N.Y. 10003

Manufactured in the USA

For Helen

Acknowledgments: American Poet (The New Mexican), Approach, The Carolina Quarterly, Castalia, Chicago Review, Epoch, The Fiddlehead, From the Hungarian Revolution (Cornell University Press), Impetus, Japan Quarterly, Midwest, The Montparnasse Review, The New York Times, On Writing, By Writers (Ginn & Co.), Parnassus, Quarterly Review of Literature, Saturday Review, Sciamachy 6, South and West, Southern Poetry Review, Southwest Review, Tri-Quarterly.

For permission to reprint "A Sheaf for Chicago," a first-prize sharer in the New "Chicago" Poem Competition, thanks are due the editors of Panorama (Chicago Daily News).

Contents

I. EAST

II. HEARTLAND

III. WEST

I. EAST

The Beachcomber

Beyond the patchwork bobbing of her back
The nineteen peaks of Sado float
In violet mist. Below, the "Exiles' Route"
Is taut with sail and net. Across
The humps of sand that blot the sea
The pinetrees hold the beaten shore,
And just as she is wasted by a cold
Necessity, the iced Siberian wind
Has bent and shriveled to their salty core.

She dreams a raft of treasure to her reach:
A silky foam will wash ten lacquered bowls
Like frozen blossoms to the beach,
And she will pluck them with a girlish hand.
Now as the sunset, like a vulgar fan,
Spreads slowly on the exiled peaks
She scoops and hurls a pebble at the waves.
But nothing happens. From those crystal founts
The frail and scattered richness never breaks.

Hearn in Matsue

That all was miniature gave him comfort
      Of a sort,
And after the Lady, Ellen Freeman,

To whom he had written finally, "Do not
      Disgust me,
Please—" the women were so otherworldly

It was like a permanent exhibition
      For which one
Scarcely had to be the connoisseur. In fact

He shut his eyes and took the nearest for both
      Bed and name
(He had tired of his); was bowed into a house

Which brushed the river a crane's cry from the
      Daimyo's Tower;
Started fussing with the garden; pushed his wife's

Few things around the room like chessmen; until,
      Pleased at last,
He braced for winter which, though wet, was very

Beautifying. He was often seen tramping from
      The bathhouse,
Flesh a-tingle, all rose against the snow.

Came time to work: a cub again, he snuffed for
      News in Old
Japan, and, stiff on haunches, englished along

With a nameless one or two, tales which drew
        The expert's
Touch like lacquered puzzle-boxes and, when solved,

Would gush from prospects charged with mountains
        Called Giraffes,
Trees tense as wire, a moon which always snared

In pineboughs, and temples which could pull one
        To the knees.
The fame did not surprise: it had awaited

Him like those fragrant ports of forty
        Years ago
The tall black hulls of home. It fit him, and he

Wore it as he felt, deservingly. What as
        Years crept by
He would not learn to bear, and ill deserved,

Was wife, friends, job, food, the too familiar
        Land itself,
And now, in winter, the Siberian wind

That tore across the sea to heap him at
        The brazier
For months, weak eyes pricked by dying charcoal.

It was then, remembering Shelley and his
        Fading coal,
He knew how much he hated all Romance.

11

Return to Hiroshima

Coming out of the station he expected
To bump into the cripple who had clomped,
Bright pencils trailing, across his dreams

For fifteen years. Before setting out
He was ready to offer both his legs,
His arms, his sleepless eyes. But it seemed

There was no need: it looked a healthy town,
The people gay, the new streets dancing
In the famous light. Even the War Museum

With its photos of the blast, the well-mapped
Rubble, the strips of blackened skin,
Moved one momentarily. After all,

From the window one could watch picnickers
Plying chopsticks as before, the children
Bombing carp with rice-balls. Finding not

What he had feared, he went home cured at last.
Yet minutes after getting back in bed
A wood leg started clomping, a thousand

Eyes leapt wild, and once again he hurtled
Down a road paved white with flesh. On waking
He knew he had gone too late to the wrong

Town, and that until his own legs numbed
And eyes went dim with age, somewhere
A fire would burn that no slow tears could quench.

12

II. PILOT

All right, let them play with it,
Let them feel all hot and righteous,
Permit them the savage joy of

Deploring my inhumanity,
And above all let them bury
Those hundred thousands once again:

I too have counted the corpses,

And say this: if Captain X
Has been martyred by the poets,
Does that mean I have to weep

Over his "moments of madness"?
If he dropped the bomb, and he did,
If I should sympathize, and I do

(I too have counted the corpses),

Has anyone created a plaint
For those who shot from that red sun
Of Nineteen Forty-One? Or

Tried to rouse just one of those
Thousand Jonahs sprawled across
The iron-whale bed of Saipan Bay?

I too have counted the corpses.

And you, Tom Staines, who got it
Huddled in "Sweet Lucy" at my side,
I still count yours, regretting

You did not last to taste the
Exultation of learning that
"Perhaps nine out of ten of us"

(I too have counted the corpses)

Would not end up as fertilizer
For next spring's rice crop. I'm no
Schoolboy, but give me a pencil

And a battlefield, and I'll make you
A formula: take one away
From one, and you've got bloody nothing.

I too have counted the corpses.

III. SURVIVORS

Of the survivors there was only one
That spoke, but he spoke as if whatever
Life there was hung on his telling all,

And he told all. Ot the three who stayed,
Hands gripped like children in a ring, eyes
Floating in the space his wall had filled,

Of the three who stayed on till the end,
One leapt from the only rooftop that
Remained, the second stands gibbering

At a phantom wall, and it's feared the last,
The writer who had taken notes, will
Never write another word. He told all.

14

The Mine: Yamaguchi

It is not hell one thinks of, however dark,
These look more weary than tormented.
One would expect, down there, a smell more human,
A noise more agonized than that raised
By cars shunted, emptied, brimmed again.

Today, remembering, the black heaps themselves
(On which conveyors drop, chip by chip,
What aeons vised and morselled to lay
A straw of light across the page)
Do not force infernal images.

After weeks of trying to forget,
The eye resists, the vision begged and gotten
Is the heart's: rows of women bent over
Feed-belts circling like blood, pickhammers
Biting at the clods that trundle by,

Raw hands flinging waste through scuttles gaped behind
While, a stone's-throw down the company road,
A smokestack grits the air with substance one
Might sniff below, or anywhere. It marks
The crematory, they pass it twice a day.

The Revolutionary

Who was it said that men to forge beyond
Must jell into a mob composed of as
Many minds, fused singly, as it has heads?

A monster-maker with a taste for blood,
He would have lumped the lot and had us
Leaping impassables, breaching impregnables.

Four hundred years before the birth of Christ,
Mencius, advisor to the King of Ch'i,
Saw man as such, and in a scarlet notebook

Laid at his liege's feet, had planted characters
So rich of seed, so thick with hate of all
That eye surveyed, the tribe of lackey scholars

Gathered by the princes to find fault,
Each weighted with a royal scythe and bearing,
In wormy fist, the straw of abuse all life's-blood

Had been spent for, fell panting across the sage's tomb.
The Chinese are a thorough, hardy race,
But the Court was overstocked with geldings,

And who, however formidable,
Could have held back those squat black ships,
Crammed to the sails with early-harvest grain,

From plying westward, port to hungry port?

Moharram

(Islam: month of mourning)

Where we ate in the canyon
The stream reflected, on the crags,
A hundred wavering heads
And the sun falling laced
The water with their blood.
When the sheep grazed down
To clatter round our fire
They wore those heads again,
And the stream had cleansed
The blood from every throat.

Yet none could feel at ease
As, catching our breath, we watched
The shepherd yelp them past
Gorged with the darkened grass.
By that afternoon of Tassua,
Stretched in a great arc of thirst,
The mourners of Hoseyn had flecked
The cragstones with their salt—
Tears, gigantic, rolled down to swell
The trickle misnamed stream.

The water was unfit to drink
And it burned the fingers where
The spits had turned in unbelievers'
Hands. When the sun went down
The sheep, dragging their puffy
Dugs, cropped past again to fold.

17

Tomorrow was Ashura, day
Of human sacrifice, not sheep's,
And blood would spatter round the gate
Of Imam Reza's Shrine.

Though safely distant, already
We could hear from the city fading
At our backs the cry of "Ya Hoseyn!"
And as on a thousand tambours
Borne as one the rough palms of mourners
Slapped against stripped chests. We bound
The spits, still smelling of our feast,
With wire, and leaving the canyon
To the dark, filed slowly down
The path those jaws had cleared.

The Woman Who Lived in a Crate

She was very famous: three times she'd sailed
    The world around
In books of photographs, pressed against the
    Imam Reza's Shrine.

Summers she would squat inside the crate,
    Cracked almsbowl up,
Ten *rials* a snapshot, jaw clenched miserably
    For an extra five.

Then as the tourist scuttled off, out poked
    Veiled head, and she
Would crawl onto the sodden road to
    Spit the money clean

And gossip with the roadsweep's mule. Guiltily
    We bore her scraps
Until we saw it was ourselves, trapped in
    Thick-walled crate, we might

Have pitied: no-one picked shamed way through
    Steaming mule-turds
To fill a leaky almsbowl, while we sat
    Tittering in the sun.

A Pipe of Opium

When I dropped to the floor
And Jahangir my friend,
Squatting above me, stuffed

The pellets in and lit them,
Enjoining me to puff,
His family started giggling.

At first euphoria of sorts,
Then a quick dissolving: Jahangir
And all his portly brood

Became an undertaker, seven-voiced,
Many fingered, and for an age
I stalked the purgatory

Of his atrocious living room,
Watching the Kerman carpet's
Garden wilt around me,

Feeling the Farsi cackle
Boom against the skull. I rose
Headachy and wiser. There are

Many ways to dodge reality,
Hundreds of states preferable
To the kind of life we own,

But the only satisfactory death
Takes us clean-lunged, clear-headed,
And very much alone.

A Persian Suite

The bulbuls do not sing here
    Anymore,
And the streambeds, dammed with silt,

Do not rise to lap the
    Scented toes
Of lovers dawdling under

Aspens with Khayyam. Am I
    Alone in
Liking it this way? It was

All too much, too much, smelling
    Of Genghis
Khan and Tamerlane. Whoever

Flung those gates apart and shoved
    A horde of
Muddy beggars through to foul

The footpaths, dip sour rags
    Into the
Pond, deserves our thanks. Now

The pond's an ossuary.
    The beggars
Do not come here anymore.

And rocking the aspens, hid
    By leaves, crows
Rain droppings, and fly on.

21

Like distressed ships they founder
      In ocean
That has never ceased to batter,

However calm the instruments
      Pronounce it,
Their arms like broken spars

Stretched for the saving pittance.
      Though the day
Be windless their rags blow wild,

And oh their mouths send out such
      Piteous
Signals, forever more the food

Must turn to garbage on the
      Painted dish.
They cry, but the fog is thick

And full of plunging monsters
      And the firm
Ships sailing by cannot shift

A sole degree from a course
      As rigid
As the Table of the Laws,

Those bent coins boiling in the wake
      Would scarcely
Fill the stomach of a gull.

III. OASIS

Nothing stands so green.
These few trees hold back
    A tide of sand

And ride the grit-blast,
Or moving with the sun,
    Which all day long

Nibbles at the grass-edge,
Twist like dervishes in
    The pool below.

Imam Reza, from all
Sides your pilgrim trails
    Stretch parched as tongues,

And chanting your name,
Balanced between water
    And death, they come.

IV. THE DOME

All gold, the pilgrims heap
Like coals beneath your
    Radiance.

Forever set, the wheeling
Sun must envy you. How
    Bright you burn!

Only the prophet, brooding
In the dark, knows you for
　　　What you are:

Bauble of Allah, how
Many sinners have purchased
　　　Peace with you?

Shall we strike the tent now,
　　　And move on
Beneath the terrible sun?

We are searchers together,
　　　You and I,
For that the world thinks madness.

Well, let them call it so!
　　　What can they
Know, those bitter ones who

Wallow on the seven shores,
　　　Of the sweet
Rush of water to the

Aching throat? Or how dream
　　　The wonder
Of need beyond fulfillment?

Enough! Again I have found
　　　Oasis
In the cool streams of your arms.

24

VI. MUEZZIN

It is a matter no longer of finding
      The most durable voice:
There are records of the best, and loudspeakers

Perch like parrots in the muezzin's cage
      Atop the minaret.
So one is not greatly stirred, being

American and here for only a year,
      By all the business
Around the Imam Reza's Shrine. Yet

Walking absurdly about at always
      Brilliant noon, one can be
Hurled to the shadows when, mincing past

The beggars at the gate, black from top
      To toe, veil bulged bonily
Over nose, eyes which see but cannot,

By God, be seen plunged to the unclean heart,
      Comes woman to her prayer.
Then let all those parrots croak together,

One's still in Persia, a thousand years ago.

II. HEARTLAND

A Sheaf for Chicago

Something queer and terrifying about Chicago: one of
the strange "centres" of the earth . . .
> D. H. Lawrence to Harriet Monroe

Always when we speak of you, we call you
Human. You are not. Nor are you any
Of the things we say: queer, terrifying.

It is the tightness of the mind that would
Confine you. No more strange than Paris
Is gay, you exist by your own laws,

Which to the millions that call you theirs,
Suffice, serve the old gargantuan needs.
Heaped as if just risen—streaming, unsmirched—

From seethings far below, you accept all.
By land, air, sea they come, certain to find
You home. For those you've once possessed, there's no

Escaping: always revealed in small
Particulars—a bar, a corner—you
Reappear complete. Even as I address

You, seeing your vastness in alleyways
And lots that fester Woodlawn, I have
A sense of islands all around, made one

By sea that feeds and spoils yet is a thing
Apart. You are that sea. And home: have
Stamped me yours for keeps, will claim me when,

Last chances spent, I wrap it up for good.
You are three million things, and each is true.
But always home. More so and more deeply

Than the sum of antheaps we have made of
You, reenter every night to dream you
Something stone can never be. And met

However far away, two that call you
Home, feel beyond the reach of words to tell
Like brothers who must never part again.

II. A CHILD IN THE CITY

In a vacant lot behind a body shop
I rooted for your heart, O city,
The truth that was a hambone in your slop.

Your revelations came as thick as bees,
With stings as smarting, wings as loud,
And I recall those towering summer days

We gathered fenders, axles, blasted hoods
To build Cockaigne and Never-never Land,
Then beat for dragons in the oily weeds.

That cindered lot and twisted auto mound,
That realm to be defended with the blood,
Became, as New Year swung around,

A scene of holocaust, where pile on pile
Of Christmas trees would char the heavens
And robe us demon-wild and genie-tall

To swirl the hell of 63rd Place,
Our curses whirring by your roofs,
Our hooves a-clatter on your face.

III. THE BALLOON

(To Auguste Piccard, his day at Soldier Field)

As you readied the balloon, tugging
At the ropes, I grabbed my father's hand.
Around us in stone tiers the others

Began to hold their breath. I watched my
Father mostly, thinking him very
Brave for toying with his pipe. Then when

You filled the giant sack with heated
Air and, waving, climbed into the
Gondola with a bunch of roses

Thrust at you, I freed my hand, cheered
And started clapping. I caught your eye,
You smiled, then left the ground. The people

Filed for exits when, twisting in
The wind, you veered above the lake, a
Pin against a thundercloud. But I

Refused to budge. My father stooped to
Beat me and cracked his precious briar
On the stone. And still I wouldn't leave.

28

He called me a young fool and dragged me,
Bawling, to the streetcar. But I couldn't
Stop watching you. I stayed up all that night,

Soaring ever higher on your star,
Through tunneled clouds and air so blue
I saw blue spots for hours. In the morning

My father laughed and said you came back down.
I didn't believe him then, and never will.
I told him I was glad he broke his pipe.

IV. THE BEACH

Even the lake repulses:
I watch them where, shellacked
        And steaming

In barbaric light, they
Huddle in their shame, the maids
        And busboys.

Even the lovers dare not
Step where the goddess rose in
        Tinted foam,

But paw each other, gape,
Spin radio dials. And hulking
        Over cards

Mothers whip strings of
Curse like lariats, jerking
        The children

29

From the shore when, suddenly
Across the beach, they hear:
    "Lost! Child lost!"

None rise. The breakers drown
Voices, radios; peak white, pound
    In like fists.

V. MESTROVIC'S INDIANS

(Equestrian statues, Michigan Avenue)

With bare heels sharp as spurs
They kick the bronze flanks of
    The horses.

But what sane beast would brave
A river wild as this, choked
    As it is

With jagged tin and all
That snarling rubber? And
    Ford to where?

Along the other bank, while the
Great arms pointing with their
    Manes convulse

In anger, the merchants
Dangle strings of gewgaws
    In the sun.

30

But no mere hoof was meant
For plunging here, and why, the
      Horses seem

To ask, would even redskins
Climb a shore where not one
      Grassblade springs?

VI. CITY OF THE WIND

All night long the lake-blast
      Rattled bones of
Dreamers in that place of glass.

Awake, they heard a roaring
      Down the lots and
Alleyways where wind flung

Rainspout, fencepost, toolshed,
      As if the town
Were tossing on the flood

Of space. All night, it seemed,
      A horde of giants
Came trampling overhead,

Tore limbs, wrenched screens, spilled
      Glass like chips of
Sky. Next day through, the dazed

31

Ones rooted in the mire,
    Then, back in beds,
Dreamt the city fairer

Than before. But how,
    Snapped antennae
Pulling roofs askew,

Autos tipped hub-deep in silt,
    Could dream raise up
What dream alone had built?

VII. EVE

In Calcutta I found her in a stall,
    A thing for sale,
Breasts like burnished gourds: some things one does
    not buy.

In Isfahan her eyes were black as wells
    Entreating alms
Of all who passed: there are deserving charities.

In Amsterdam above a darkened street
    A bay window
Framed her sundries, proffering bliss: I was not sold.

In Seville she wore a gypsy shawl and
    Bangles on her
Dancing feet: the silver dropped around them was not
    mine.

In Paris she hugged me down the avenue,
    Skirt a jocund
Sail, towed by the dollars in my purse: I tacked for
    home.

32

In Chicago she waits behind a door
        No common key
Can budge: who enters there will never get away

VIII. THE GANG

One can hardly extricate them
From the props they lounge against,
Or see them for the smoke lips

Link in chains that will not hold.
At night the sound of pennies tossed
Upon the sidewalk-cracks is like

A slowly breaking mirror
Which reflects the little that they
Are. What girl dare pass and not

Be whistled at? Their appraisements
Are quick, absolute: that water
Freezes into ice needs scant

Deliberation. Whatever
The day sweeps up, their sole
Antagonist is boredom, which

By merely standing around, they
Thwart at every turn but one.
They scorn whom others envy,

The man who ambles by, duty
Snapping at the heels, and should lovers
Cross, there is a sudden flinging down

(By eyes so starved, they almost moan)
And then a coupling in the dust.
Allow them such years to lean

And wait. Soon they must approach
The selfsame corner, and hail
The gang that is no longer there.

IX. THE NEIGHBORHOOD

Long away, I find it pure
Exotic; no matter that they roll
The sidewalks up at ten and boys

Want height to leap for basketballs:
It is a place, and there are corners
Where one does what one would do.

Come back, I find the expected
Changes: shabby streets grown shabbier,
The mob all scattered, old girl friends

Losing more of what's been lost,
The supermarts turned up like sows
To give the brood of grunters suck,

And Mother, like a thickening tree
Whose roots work deeper as the woodman
Nears, spread over all, the wind which sweeps

Across her whispering "Stay On."
Two weeks of that, and there are
Other whispers that I heed.

The train pulls in and I descend,
To mount before it pulls away.
Goodby Mother, goodby! I'm off

Again to Someplace Else, where
Chafing together once a month
The strangers sit and write sweet letters home.

III. WEST

Notes for a Guidebook

In celestial Padua
The ghosts walk hugely
In the public squares.

Donatello is one,
His horseman in the
Piazza San Antonio
Guards the gruff saint's heart
Like a mystic ruby,
The ears of the horse,
Of the rider,
Riddled by prayer.

Giotto, Dante are others,
The painter's frescoes
Float like clouds
Above the city,
The poet's cantos
Ring upon its walls.

And what of us,
Who stand with heads
Strained back, feet tapping?
Shall we eat, sleep,
Be men again?
Shall we slip back
To the whores of Venice?—
Dwarfs, clods, motes of dust
In the brightness.

The Fountain of Ammannati

(Piazza della Signoria, Florence)

Below the pigeon-spotted seagod
The mermen pinch the mermaids,
And you shopgirls eat your food.

No sneak-vialed aphrodisiac
Can do—for me, for you—what
Mermen pinching mermaids in a whack

Of sunlit water can. And do.
These water-eaten shoulders and these thighs
Shall glisten though your gills go blue,

These bones will never clatter in the breath.
My dears, before your dust swirls either up
Or down—confess: this world is richly wet.

And consider: there is a plashless world
Outside this stream-bright square
Where girls like you lie curled

And languishing for love like mine.
And you were such as they
Until ten sputtering jets began

To run their ticklish waters down your
Spine. Munch on, my loves, you are but
Sun-bleached maidens in a world too poor

To tap the heart-wells that would flow,
And flow. You are true signorine
Of that square where none can go

And then return. Where dusty mermen
Parch across a strand of sails and spars,
And dream of foamy thighs that churn.

Torero

Some see him dancer,
Delight as the banderillas
Hit and quiver from his practiced hand,
Fall like a savage
Bird, piece by piece, talons piercing,
Yet there are those
Who cheer him as compassionate butcher,
Sniff the wild flesh on the hospital table,
Marvel as sharp ribs expand, hunger
Fades from the eyes of widows and orphans.

Others see him priest,
Pray as he sights along the sword,
Hosanna as he plunges toward the altar,
See the swordhilt as
Chalice spilling hot as flame, take the host
Of the ears, the tail,
While he circles the arena
And is pelted by hats, fans, a hundred
Twisted flowers. As the dead bull
Is dragged along the sand, these cross themselves.

And there are some
Who see great panniers choked
With easy pesetas, their gambler hearts
Choking with love
As he kneels before the bull, spreads glistering arms:

Only the torero,
Sad face stiff with fear, sees the bull.
Beyond the shrines in cheap hotels, the heaped pesetas.
The villa by the sea,—horns
Like a fist of knives brush him in the dark.

In a Spanish Garden

Aranjuez, he remembered waking—
Jardin de la Isla. He lay
All night among the trampled roses
And high above him now
The one-armed faun, features haggard
In the dewy light, stared down
Like a conqueror. Somewhere
At his back a fountain dripped.

He sat up dazed and, groping round,
Snatched and shook the bottle
Like a club. The goatboy did not budge.
The fountain kept on dripping,
The scent of roses was as sour
As puke. And as he moved up
To the hedge, those little mouths
Were snapping at his heels.

Straddling the hedge, he whooped and toppled
Headlong to the path when, popping
From a lilac bush, he saw a pitchfork
Then a beard. Such screams pierced
All around him, the very leaves
Screwed up to buds again. And then
It was he heard the pounding of
A thousand hoofs upon wet gravel.

He scrambled up the ornamental gate
And, rocking there, watched until
He thought him blind the pitchforks flashing
At his feet like waves. He whooped again
And kicked his heels into the bars
Like bronco ribs. And then he cried—
Your bloody roses! *Caramba!*
If this is Eden, where the hell is God?

The Road from Delphi

The twin prophetic streams still running through
Our heads, we drank above the gorge and watched
The eagles. You remembered, as sunset
Forged a halo over you and stained
The clear wine red, the country's tragedy.
Too much history, I said, erodes the best of lands.

Yet passing Thebes again, this time in darkness,
You spoke of Oedipus, his darkness,
And now the rattling of the bus became
The work of furies. I smiled knowingly
But envied the cunning of your sex
Which makes of the flintiest peak a roost in time.

Escale

One remembers a port where boats
      Tap fitfully
Against wharf-poles and wharf-side shops,

Patched awnings taut, are cool as
      Sunlit fathoms.
At times the rooftops of the town

Swim like brilliant shoals the washed
      And briny air.
One remembers a bar where fish-soup's

On all hours and sailors wait the
      Windfall virgins
Of long sea-rocked nights. There, on a

Shimmered terrace, steeped in acrid
      Afternoons, they
Lean across the tables, burning,

To watch years slip like freighters
      Down the seaways.
And there remain, knowing the worst

Of inland days, the rot, the sloth,
      The ennui, to
Tramp in dream the unmarked shore.

Chekhov in Nice

Along the Boulevard des Anglais
Tourists mistook him for Lautrec,
Though he was taller
And when not hunched over hacking
His walk was straight enough.

Perhaps it was the way he stared
At women, like a beggar
At a banquet window, and then
He was always scrabbling for a notebook
While the snickering revelers

Flowed like water round a stone.
Oh they all knew him artist.
All, that is, except the people
He would talk to in his
Scant atrocious French: the waiter,

The cabdriver, the man who
Brought his boots back in the morning
Like an oblation to Apollo.
To them he was a munificent
White Russian, title snatched,

A parcel of serfs languishing
For his return. Certainly
He was unhappy. And the chambermaids
Were touched by nailmarks
Through the blood-flecks on his sheet.

The century had just turned over,
And the Côte was never gayer.
Even the dowagers, strapped
To beachchairs all along the shore,
Felt young again and very beautiful.

And rather scornful, he was quick
To see, of the old-young man
Who moved among them like a noctambule,
His back to Mother Russia,
Seagulls screaming at his ears.

II

He had just turned forty, and now
At times he felt himself regretting.
Oh they had expected far too much
Of one as sick and poor, hung with
Unmarried sisters and a widowed dam.

Wasn't it enough to have planted
The usual imaginary garden?
Must he also, like some poet,
Sing upon the ruddy boughs?
Were he less the son, he'd have come

Here twenty years ago. Before those
Germs, swarming, had carved
A kingdom of his chest, before
The flame had risen from his bowels
To fan within his head. Were he less the son . . . .

44

And the reputation, so harshly won,
Did precious little good in France.
Who'd risk displeasing one who'd make of her,
However high her beauty,
A thing of pity in some dismal tale?

Foutu! he muttered as he slunk
Back to his room and tossed his hat
Upon the pile of doodled papers
On the desk. Now he longed for home.
In the few years left to him

Would come—was bound to come—
Another thirty stories and a dozen plays.
Then no doubt they'd prop his bones
Between those giants in Novo-Devechy.
But were there any choice to make, he'd act

The part of one the world was still applauding,
That country squire of his,
Petulant, bored, pining for the Côte d'Azur,
And—if one could believe those Russian hacks—
Likely to live forever.

Words on a Windy Day

Airing out the clothes,
    The odor of mothballs
        Driving me inside,
I watch in wonder
    As the wind fills
        Trouserlegs and sweaters,

Whips them light and dark.
    In that frayed coat
        I courted her a year,
In that old jacket
    Married her, then brushed
        Her tears off with a sleeve.

The wind blows through them,
    Tosses them about,
        These mildewed ghosts of love
That life, for lack of something
    Simple as a clothespin,
        Let fall, one by one.

The Rock

Year after year he returned to the same
Spot, hoping for a change. But found
No change, except that sometimes
The water was darker, sometimes
The beach was littered, sometimes not.

Month after month he thought as he
Imagined the journey back,
This time all will be different,
This time the rock will stand free,
Pushed back the shrouding sea.

But always, except that sometimes
The water tossed darker, sometimes
As light as cloud, the sea
Would reach the place on the rock
His head had dashed with blood.

And this distressed him. For
If the sea was changeless,
Except for the color, except for
The look of the beach, he was not.
As he saw when bent across

The rock, his face a scum upon
The moving water. Yet year
After year he came back to look again,
Until the bloodstain on the rock
Was like a sleeping eye, washed

By the hissing foam, until they had
To hold him as he scraped across
The sand. Dropping their pails
Below the rock like explorers
Come to the one and only place.

And made a castle there beside
The rock. Year after year
The grandchildren returned, and saw
The water lapping on the rock,
And thought of him, and thought of death.